Original title:
Beneath the Roof of Home

Copyright © 2025 Creative Arts Management OÜ
All rights reserved.

Author: Ryan Sterling
ISBN HARDBACK: 978-1-80587-061-6
ISBN PAPERBACK: 978-1-80587-531-4

Resting in the Unseen

In my chair, I snooze away,
Dreams of snacks lead me astray.
Cats on laps with tiny paws,
Listen close, they plot their claws.

Lost in thoughts of yesterday,
That last cookie slipped away.
A creaky floor becomes my foe,
When I snack as if in slow-mo.

The Sentiment of Safety

Shower curtains wave and sway,
Like a superhero ballet.
Socks that march, a funny pair,
Keep my toes from frigid air.

Couch cushions hide my secret stash,
Of chocolate bars and crumbs — oh, splash!
Pajamas worn all day, no doubt,
Who needs fashion when I'm about?

Explorations in the Attic

Dusty boxes filled with tales,
Chasing ghosts like quirky snails.
A long-lost hat from '93,
Claims it's still in style – just wait and see!

Old toys whisper, 'Play with me!'
While spider webs make their decree.
Every trip brings a treasure trove,
Of laughter where memories rove.

Pillars of Comfort

Chairs that squeak, they know my name,
A cushion fort – it's quite the game.
Pizza boxes stacked with glee,
Decorate my victory spree.

Silly socks with polka dots,
Help me dance in funny spots.
Home's a stage for our charades,
Where laughter never ever fades.

The Rhythm of Evening Chores

Dust bunnies dance, oh what a sight,
Mop and broom take the stage tonight.
Socks on the floor perform their own tune,
Laundry baskets hum their cliché monsoon.

Dishes clatter, a symphony loud,
Spatulas waving, they're ever so proud.
In the chaos, a dog steals a shoe,
Who knew chores could be this funny too?

Fireside Confessions

By the fire, secrets spill freely,
Not just the beans, but the snacks we eat greedily.
Grandpa's tales grow taller each night,
Was he really a knight? Or just out of sight?

A marshmallow ghost hovers in the air,
As we laugh at Aunt Betty's crazy hair.
Stories twist, tongues sometimes trip,
What's real and what's just a comic script?

Scents of Seasoned Love

In the kitchen, aromas collide,
Garlic and herbs take us for a ride.
Burnt toast wafts like a perfume divine,
A twist of fate, just another design.

Pasta bubbles while we concoct,
Saucy mishaps, it's love that we've locked.
With every burnt bite, we giggle and cheer,
In this culinary love, there's never a fear.

Unfinished Conversations

We chat over dinner, forks in a dance,
Lost in stories, we miss our chance.
'What was I saying?' becomes our refrain,
As the cat steals my food to add to the gain.

Mom's witty quips float on the air,
Each punchline swallowed in laughter rare.
Outside, rib-tickling crickets join in,
What was once serious becomes our best win!

Echoes of Laughter

In the kitchen, pots bang loud,
A recipe for chaos, I'm so proud.
Cat leaps high, dog is a blur,
Spaghetti's flying, what a fur!

Socks on the ceiling, I start to wonder,
Did the dryer conspire, is it pulling thunder?
Dishes shrink while I cook in haste,
Mealtime dinners, a slapstick taste.

Windows to Warmth

Through the glass, the sun's a glow,
Neighbor's dog barks; I'm the show.
Curtains dance like they've got glee,
Who knew a breeze would bring such spree?

Tea spills, while dancing feet,
Try to tango on the carpet, sweet.
Our reflections join the fun parade,
What a spectacle this home has made!

Foundations of Belonging

Cracks in the wall tell tales of old,
Jokes exchanged when the night is cold.
We trip on toys, and laughter bursts,
Stumbling joy, a love that thrusts.

Chairs creak like they hold a sage,
Each room's a stage, each flip a page.
Memories pile up, gifts from the past,
In this silly circus, we'll ever last.

Secrets in the Attic

Dusty boxes, what treasures await!
Forgotten relics, don't tempt fate.
Skeletons dance in my head, oh dear,
Grandma's old hat makes me cheer!

Old toys whisper, stories unfold,
A ghostly raccoon in the corner bold.
Between the nets and the faded quilts,
Laughter's woven through ancient silt.

The Scent of Home-Cooked Meals

In the kitchen, pots go clang,
And granddad's recipes are sang.
A pinch of salt, a dash of spice,
Where laughter simmers, oh so nice.

Mom's secret sauce, a note to frame,
Uncle's stories spark the flame.
The dog in wait, with hopeful eyes,
Dreams of meaty, tasty pies.

Cousins compete for the last bite,
As plates get cleared, we still delight.
The smoke alarm, it's quite a show,
Who burned the toast? We'll never know!

Dinner ends with games galore,
A dance-off, then we hit the floor.
In our haven, joy's the theme,
With every meal, we laugh and beam.

Moments Frozen in Time

Snapshots hanging on the wall,
Of goofy grins and epic falls.
Grandma's hair, a purple hue,
She claims it's just a style brand new.

Dad in shorts, a fashion crime,
Mowing the lawn, he's lost in rhyme.
We laugh about his disco days,
And shake our heads in warm displays.

Siblings bickering, oh what a sight,
The wrestling match that lasted all night.
In our fortress, silly tales bloom,
Where chaos dances, erasing gloom.

With every glance, a chuckle shared,
In our gallery, love is bared.
Captured moments, so sublime,
With every frame, we laugh in time.

The Quilt of Our Lives

Stitched together with laughter's thread,
Colors of chaos, love widespread.
Each patch a story, slightly frayed,
Memories linger, none betrayed.

A block for each of our friends,
Silly arguments that never ends.
The stains of snacks, a badge of pride,
We snicker at the times we tried.

Raindrops tapped a rhythm sweet,
While we huddled, our hearts in beat.
With every stitch, a tale we weave,
In this fabric of life, we believe.

A blanket hug when days are long,
In our sanctuary, we belong.
The quilt wraps us, both snug and tight,
Knit with humor, our hearts ignite.

From Childhood to Maturity

In a treehouse, hidden from view,
We'd plot adventures, me and you.
Wielding swords made from sticks and dreams,
In our kingdom, nothing's as it seems.

Time flew by like a kite at play,
We grew taller, day by day.
Now we sip tea, and roll our eyes,
At youthful schemes and wildest lies.

From bike rides down the winding lane,
To late-night snacks that brought us fame.
We traded candies for serious talks,
Still cracking jokes on evening walks.

Though years may flash like fireflies,
Those silly days, they never die.
In this journey, side by side,
We laugh at the waves, and with the tide.

Lullabies of the Past

In the corner, Grandma snores,
While the cat plots and roars.
We tiptoe past with snacks in hand,
Whispered giggles, the best of plans.

Old stories swirl like dusty dust,
"Do not touch that!" is a must.
Yet the secret stash is all our own,
Where giggles turn to ice cream cones.

The echoes of laughs fill each room,
As toys create a cheerful boom.
With every creak and every hue,
Tomorrow's tales await anew.

Under blankets, we all hide,
A fortress built, with hearts so wide.
While shadows dance and fingers trace,
The warmth of love, our favorite space.

Revelations in the Rooms

In the kitchen, cookies burn,
Dad is lost in a cookbook's turn.
Mom glances over, rolling her eyes,
"Just order pizza; it's a surprise!"

The living room, a mess of fun,
Where socks become the target run.
The dog joins in, with barks and leaps,
Who knew laundry could cause such peeps?

Bedtime stories turn to quests,
As pillows morph into dragon nests.
With every chapter, yawns arise,
Yet we still chase the moonlit skies.

In the hallway, secrets exchanged,
A brother's tale slightly rearranged.
But laughter echoes, nothing's amiss,
In rooms of warmth, we find our bliss.

Steps that Dance with Joy

On the stairs, we march in line,
Imitating Dad, he's doing just fine.
But Mom joins in, twirls without shame,
In this goofy, sweet family game.

We shuffle through the kitchen beat,
Spinning around on wobbly feet.
The dog's confused; he joins the dance,
As we laugh hard and take a chance.

Old records play, the tunes go wild,
Grandpa grooves, like a happy child.
Mom tries to lead with two left feet,
But all we see is her dazzling sweet.

As night falls, we waltz on air,
Bumping into walls, without a care.
With every misstep, joy does grow,
In our raucous, twirling show.

Fragments of Family

Family photos line the wall,
Grandma's wig, a funny sprawl.
A cousin dressed as a spooky ghost,
Laughter brewing as we toast.

Holidays bring out the crazed,
Uncle Bob in pajamas, amazed.
Silly hats, and stories unfold,
In snapshots where fun is retold.

Board games spark a fierce debate,
While our puppy thinks it's all first-rate.
Who needs to win when laughter's the prize?
With rolling eyes and cake-covered thighs.

A dining table filled with cheer,
Where every bite brings family near.
In every crumb and spilled delight,
Fragments of us shine really bright.

The Open Door Surprise

A knock on the door, who could it be?
A cat with a hat, as silly as can be.
He struts in the room, like he owns the place,
With a twirl of his tail, he's a furry disgrace.

The dog gives a bark, oh what a surprise!
This party's a circus, oh my, oh my!
They dance on the rug, leading quite the show,
With paws in the air, they steal the flow.

Mom walks in, and oh, what a sight!
Two pets in a tango, such pure delight.
She stifles a giggle, a grin on her face,
These creatures, these jesters, they brighten the space.

So here's to the laughter, and joy that they bring,
In a house full of chaos, we all learn to sing.
With doors left ajar, and the silliness shared,
Home is a playground, where no one is scared.

The Backbone of Belonging

In the kitchen, a flurry, a dance with the pots,
Mom's cooking up trouble, with flour in knots.
Dad's at the table, his jokes flying high,
A sandwich un-sandwiched, oh me, oh my!

Sister bursts in, wielding spoons like a sword,
She claims she's the chef, it's too much to afford.
Her pancake creations, a sight to behold,
With sprinkles and jelly, they shine like gold.

Brother jumps in with a wink and a grin,
He masters the art of pancake spin.
But one flip too many sends batter on walls,
The laughter erupts, and the kitchen enthralls.

Here in our chaos, we find our sweet calm,
Between spills and giggles, we sip our warm balm.
Together we thrive, in our quirky old den,
The heart of it all, is the love we defend.

Home is What We Make It

With tape and some cardboard, we build a great fort,
Teddy bears gather, all ready for sport.
We place down a rug, it's our royal domain,
King-sized adventures, atop plush terrain.

Elbows and knees in a mess of the game,
A battle of wits, oh, what a shame!
With capes made from towels, we dash to the door,
Yet tripping on slippers sends us to the floor.

Mom peeks on in, she can't help but tease,
"You kids are wild creatures, do you ever know ease?"
But laughter erupts, as we leap in delight,
This home full of love makes everything right.

So treasure the madness, the joy that we share,
In the quirks of our life, you'll find love everywhere.
For magic is real in the mess and the fun,
Home is what we make it, together as one.

Sanctuary's Embrace

In pjs stretched, we take a stand,
A fortress built from scattered toys.
The cat's the prince, we're just the band,
Our laughter echoes, muffling noise.

With snacks in hand, we charge the fort,
On couch cushions, our soldiers lie.
Each pillow's thrown, we hold the court,
The dog just sighs, and wonders why.

In battles fierce, we spill the juice,
The floor is lava, don't touch ground.
With sprightly moves, we've made our truce,
Our kingdom's chaos knows no bound.

As twilight comes, we end the game,
The rug's our map, the dreamers dream.
In this wild land, we're all the same,
In giggles shared, we find our beam.

Whispers of the Hearth

In kitchen's heat, the pies take flight,
The oven hums a gentle tune.
We swirl and twirl, the flour's white,
Bakers united—please don't swoon.

The dog has claimed the chef's old hat,
While pots and pans perform a dance.
A sprinkle here, a little splat,
Each bite a tale—of luck and chance.

Dad's jokes rise with the rising bread,
"Put on your shoes; they're getting stale!"
With rolling pins, we forge ahead,
Against the odds, we will not fail.

In crumbs and laughter, love is spun,
This kitchen's heart beats loud and bright.
A noisy gang, but oh, what fun,
With every meal, we spark delight.

The Heart Nestled Within

In blankets piled, we build a cave,
Our laughter spills like hot cocoa,
With every pop, a silly wave,
Who threw the snack? We do not know.

In tangled cords and games of hide,
The fridge hums softly, a lullaby.
With whispers sweet, we bide our time,
The clock ticks slow; oh, me oh my.

When midnight strikes, the giggles rise,
We stealthily raid the chip stash bare.
With crumbs on cheeks and sleepy eyes,
A secret pact—just one more dare.

As morning light begins to creep,
The blanket fort starts to feel alive.
We'll laugh all day and skip our sleep,
In hijinks found, our hearts will thrive.

Shadows in the Hallway

In hallway's light, we creep like spies,
With flashlights bright, we start our quest.
The dog is chief, with keenest eyes,
To find the snack drawer, we're obsessed.

Each corner hides a tale untold,
As shadows dance upon the wall.
With giggles loud, we're brave and bold,
Our mission's clear: to seek, to haul.

A sock thrown here, a shoe misplaced,
The chaos reigns like windy gusts.
We brave the night, with snacks embraced,
In whispered schemes, it's just a must.

With laughter ringing down the hall,
Each step a game, each breath a thrill.
In shadows play, we feel so small,
Yet in this space, we find our will.

A Hearth of Memories

The couch is a throne where I reign supreme,
Popcorn in hand, lost in a dream.
The dog steals my snacks, I just roll my eyes,
In the kingdom of comfort, where laughter flies.

Cats perched high, like silent spies,
Plotting their takeovers with sly little sighs.
The fridge hums a tune, it's not much to boast,
But in this circus, I'm the happy host.

Footsteps in the Corridor

The hallway echoes with my shuffles and slides,
Chasing the kids as they giggle and hide.
A misplaced shoe trip—oh, it's part of the fun,
I'll get back at them with tickles when I'm done.

Each squeaky floorboard, a tale it could tell,
Of midnight snacks and wild games that went well.
With every jump, there's a ruckus and cheer,
An obstacle course, that's the mission this year!

Windows to the Soul

With curtains drawn wide, the sun's got a show,
It dances on floors, around toys in a row.
The neighbors peek in, I pretend they can't see,
Doing the cha-cha while sipping my tea.

Birds are my audience, perched on the sill,
Cawing their laughter, give me a thrill.
I wave like a madman, they flutter away,
I'm the quirky performer in this bright cabaret!

The Embrace of Comfort

Socks with holes? They're my lucky charm,
A blanket burrito keeps me nice and warm.
The world outside fades, it's cocoon time galore,
In this cuddle fortress, who could ask for more?

The silence is peaceful, except for the snore,
Of granddad who naps, epic tales about war.
As I sit with my ice cream, giggles escape,
In this haven of laughter, we're all in great shape.

Nooks of Solace

In the corner, socks unfold,
A fortress made of laundry, bold.
Dust bunnies play, a merry crew,
In the chaos, laughter grew.

Couches whisper secrets, sweet,
Where snacks are found, oh what a treat!
The cat's on watch, a royal king,
For mischief lies in everything.

Chairs dance lightly, creaks and groans,
As we debate our favorite scones.
Coffee spills, a wild cascade,
Yet joy's the price we gladly paid.

Toys sprout legs and start a race,
Pillows become a cozy space.
We dive into the cushions deep,
And find the treasures we will keep.

Love's Quiet Corner

In the nook where shadows play,
A sandwich waits, but it's gone astray.
Mismatched socks in tender clumps,
Sing sweetly of our lazy jumps.

The lamp winks, a cheeky grin,
As stories spark and laughter spins.
A rug that once was pristine blue,
Now stuffed with crumbs from snacks we chewed.

Tea mugs float, their saucers lost,
In this haven, we don't count the cost.
Love keeps the chaos, hand in hand,
In our corner, life is grand.

The clock ticks on, but no one cares,
Time plays tricks as laughter shares.
In our island of warmth and cheer,
Every moment feels like a year.

The Rhythm of Familiarity

Walls hum a tune of pot and pan,
As the dog decides what's part of the plan.
Footsteps dance on creaky steps,
With socks that hide in oozy depths.

Dishes sing, a clattering choir,
While spilled milk sets the mood on fire.
We argue about who did the deed,
Yet love ties tight, fulfilling the need.

The fridge door creaks, a ghostly sound,
It opens wide, treasures abound.
Leftovers tell a tale of cheer,
In this rhythm, we hold dear.

Jokes bounce off these painted walls,
As laughter echoes in joyful calls.
Each tick and tock adds to the score,
In our home, there's always more.

Gardens of Grace

In the garden, weeds dance with pride,
Sunflowers grin as bees collide.
Trowels play hide and seek like friends,
While laughter in the breeze transcends.

The hose sprays back, a slippery foe,
As kids run wild, stealing the show.
In muddy boots, adventures bloom,
With flowers giggling to chase the gloom.

The gnomes gossip while evening falls,
Their painted eyes become the walls.
Petunias tease the daisies bright,
In this garden, all feels right.

Sunsets spill their colors bold,
As we reminisce tales retold.
In the heart of chaos, we find our place,
In these joyful, tangled gardens of grace.

Tides of Togetherness

In the kitchen, crumbs do roam,
A dance of chaos, it's my home.
Pasta flops and sauces splatter,
Laughter spills, it's all that matters.

The laundry spins with socks askew,
Matching pairs? Oh, that'll do!
Tiny hands, they tug and tease,
Life's a maze, yet still we please.

The dog jumps high, the cat just stares,
Board games lead to playful airs.
We argue loud, we laugh and hug,
In this whirlwind, we're so snug.

From make-believe to snack attacks,
Family love fills in the cracks.
Through ups and downs, we gently wade,
Together, messes do cascade.

Echoes in the Quiet

In the stillness, a sneeze erupts,
A silent room? No way, corrupt!
The cat's on guard, the dog makes noise,
What's their secret? Oh, pure joys!

When silence hovers, think again,
The kids are plotting, it's a game.
Under the table, their giggles flare,
A ghostly knight? Or just a chair?

With popcorn trails across the floor,
The couch's cushions are a door.
Who needs the peace and quiet nice,
When chaos serves its own device?

In echoes of their playful schemes,
Lies the laughter, love, and dreams.
For every sound has a tale to tell,
In this quiet, we thrive so well.

Where Time Stands Still

In the corner, the clock has stalled,
Time forgot, or maybe called.
Coffee brewed, but never sipped,
The hours fly while we just tripped.

The dog's on guard, the cat's a blur,
Chasing shadows, that's the spur!
As we trip over shoes and toys,
The world outside? Oh, joy oh joy!

From cereal fights to pillow forts,
We plan adventures, wild retorts.
The world can wait, it's no big deal,
With giggles shared, that's the real meal.

In this mish-mash, we find our thrill,
Where each second slows to a chill.
With hearts aligned and faces bright,
Here, every moment feels just right.

Seasons Under One Sky

Spring brings puddles, so much fun,
We splash and laugh, under the sun.
Summer's heat with ice cream drips,
A sticky mess, but what fun trips!

Autumn leaves, they swirl and spin,
We rake them up, but where to begin?
Kids dive in with squeals of glee,
Amongst the crunch, it's pure esprit!

Winter's blankets, soft and white,
Snowman battles become the fight.
Hot cocoa spills from cups so wide,
With marshmallow snowballs, we take pride!

Each season brings a quirky cheer,
Together we have all we hold dear.
Under the sky, we find our bliss,
In every giggle, we reminisce.

Shadows of a Distant Dawn

In the kitchen, coffee brews,
The toast jumps, with all due dues.
Cats playing hide-and-seek with time,
While socks are lost in their own rhyme.

Pancakes flip like acrobats,
Butter melts; what are those spats?
Family circus spreads its cheer,
With sticky fingers drawing near.

All the world's a stage it seems,
With mismatched shoes and silly dreams.
Who knew breakfast could be this grand?
In a house where joy has planned.

Even the tupperware doth sing,
As lids and leftovers twist and cling.
A loud laugh bursts, rolling like a ball,
In this chaos, we embrace it all.

Echoes of Laughter

In the hallway, giggles ring,
As siblings plot their sneaky fling.
With whispered jokes and playful shoves,
Creating chaos, wrapped in loves.

Dinner time is a wild spree,
Like racing horses, can't you see?
Forks are swords, and food's the quest,
In this home, we feel so blessed.

The walls can tell a tale or two,
Of all our antics and what we do.
From spilled juice to prank-filled days,
Our memories sparkle in funny ways.

Cushions tossed like fluffy bombs,
Do you hear the laughter, the joyful psalms?
In this echo, where joy is a song,
We find our peace, we all belong.

Under the Eaves

Up in the attic, treasures unfold,
A dusty bicycle, stories told.
Cobwebbed corners hide a surprise,
As dad fits into his old size.

Mice chuckle at our brave attempts,
To keep the past and its pretense.
With each box, nostalgia's call,
We stumble and trip, but we still crawl.

In the corner, an old clown suit,
With floppy shoes that still compute.
Hiding laughter, we dance around,
As old ghosts cheer with playful sound.

The eaves creak beneath our feet,
With every laugh, our hearts compete.
In this castle of smiles and glee,
We write stories of our family tree.

Sanctuary of Dreams

The living room, a stage for fun,
With pillows flying, smiles to shun.
Fortresses built from random stuff,
In this chaos, life is enough.

Remote control is a famous wand,
With silly voices, we're all fond.
A movie night that turns to play,
As popcorn flies in giggles' array.

Napping cats are our peacekeepers,
While children dream of daring leapers.
With every snore, a tale is spun,
A symphony of dreams begun.

Beneath each blanket, joy's delight,
As dusk bikes up to meet the night.
In this quirky bungle we call home,
Laughter echoes in every dome.

The Pulse of a Family

In the kitchen, chaos reigns,
Spaghetti sticks to the ceiling,
Laughter echoes through the halls,
While the dog steals our dinner feelings.

Mom's yelling, 'Where's my phone?',
Dad's lost in the fridge again,
Siblings fighting for the remote,
It's family life — our beautiful mess, amen!

The cat jumps, the baby squeals,
A dance-off breaks out in the den,
We slide on the hardwood floors,
Making memories like kids again.

Each hug is a slightly damp hug,
With spilled juice and sticky hands,
In this circus of love and noise,
We find joy in our mismatched bands.

Windowsill Gardens

On the sill, plants wave and droop,
Sunflowers dance to the beat,
Dad waters them like a crazy troop,
With hopes they'll bloom and not just cheat.

Mom's mint grows wild, it deserves a prize,
She claims it calms her crazy thoughts,
Little do we know it's a disguise,
To mask the chaos we never fought.

The basil pot is on its third revival,
We treat it like our family pet,
It's more 'what's for dinner' survival,
Than a fancy meal — you can bet!

With every sprout, a story's brewed,
Like the siblings in our house — so spry,
These little plants, they share their mood,
In windowed hopes, we reach for the sky.

Embraces and Farewells

In the hallway, bags are packed tight,
Each farewell's a game of charades,
Mom hugs the school books with delight,
While Dad swears he'll miss our escapades.

Sister's off to dance in high heels,
Brother claims he'll be next in line,
Each goodbye, wrapped in meal deals,
As we giggle and pretend it's fine.

With snacks stuffed in every pocket,
We race for the door in a fray,
"Who forgot the keys?" — it's always a shock it,
As the timer counts down, "Hurry! You'll be late!"

Yet, when night falls under this roof,
Each hug reminds us where we belong,
In this whirlwind of love and goof,
We sing our family's silly song.

The Path to Our Roots

Our backyard holds secrets untold,
Where we dig for treasures and moles,
Mom shouts, "That's a worm, not gold!",
While Dad builds forts with questionable roles.

Treehouses rise like dreams on high,
We leap with courage from the limbs,
"Superman can fly!" we shout to the sky,
Though gravity recalls our whims.

Grass stains mark our wild retreat,
As we tumble and roll with glee,
No path too tough for our little feet,
Adventure awaits — just wait and see!

Our family's laughter is the compass,
Guiding us through each little quest,
With giggles, we happily combust,
Creating memories, we are truly blessed.

The Glow of Evening Light

When the sun starts to dip, it's a sight,
Cats dance in shadows, oh what a delight!
A dog's sneaky crawl, on tiptoe he creeps,
While laughter erupts as the blender beeps.

Footsteps echo like ghosts on the floor,
Mom in her slippers, she's out to explore.
Dad's munching popcorn, a crunch every chews,
As we giggle and snicker, dodging his snooze.

The clock ticks away, but we're still in the zone,
With games and with giggles, we call it our own.
The glow of the evening, ignites up the room,
With humor and love, dispelling all gloom.

Corners of Serenity

In a cozy nook, I find my retreat,
A cat on my lap, oh, isn't life sweet?
With socks on my hands, I sip from my bowl,
Who knew a fruit salad could lighten the soul?

Books stacked so high, they're a tower of cheer,
Each one's a story I hold ever dear.
Mom's craft supplies explode like a fight,
With glitter and glue, she's a magnificent sight!

Then a quiet "oops" when the cat's makes a mess,
Feathers and yarn, oh the feline success!
In corners of laughter, serenity gleams,
As we nurture our hope in the land of dreams.

Moments on the Stairs

Each step is a pathway to giggles and fun,
Down we tumble like a rolling bun.
In a race to the bottom, we leap like a hare,
Landing in laughter, with hugs to spare.

Mom calls it chaos, we call it our game,
An obstacle course, it's never the same!
With pillows and blankets, we craft mighty forts,
In moments on stairs, we hold royal courts.

Dad's on the couch, navigating his dreams,
While we trip over shoes, plot twists, and schemes.
With grins and with giggles, we are quite the pair,
In hilarious moments, we float through the air.

Letters in the Loft

In the dusty old loft, secrets unwind,
Old letters reveal the peculiar kind.
Grandpa's old jokes, they tickle us pink,
With puns and with riddles, we stop and we think.

A treasure map drawn with crayons and flair,
Leads to the cookies, now that's not unfair!
Then a riddle about socks, how do they flee?
With a wiggle and giggle, they ran off from me!

As we peek through the boxes, surprises abound,
In letters and laughter, our joy knows no bound.
With voices so merry, we raise up a cheer,
For memories stacked high—and a little more gear!

Sheltered from the Storm

The rain is tapping at the door,
Puddles forming on the floor.
We laugh and dance, a silly sight,
In socks that never match just right.

Dad's umbrella's now a hat,
Mom's soup's too hot—just like the cat.
We leap and dodge as thunder rolls,
While inside we share our funny goals.

A storm outside, but joy within,
With silly games, our favorite kin.
We roast the marshmallows on the stove,
Who knew indoor camping would feel like a trove?

Laughter echoes, shadows play,
In this shelter, we find our way.
Through storms we stick, our bonds don't sever,
As long as we're together, we're clever forever.

Flickers of Yesterday

In boxes stacked, dust dances light,
Old photos show our biggest fright.
Mom in curlers, Dad in his shorts,
Captured moments turn into retorts.

The hairdos scream from days long past,
We giggle over memories cast.
A dance-off from the living room,
Where Grandpa shows us all his moves.

Nostalgia flickers, a fun parade,
Each story shared makes laughter cascade.
We dress up silly, like the past,
In costume chaos, we free our blast.

A treasure chest of funny times,
With each laugh, the joy climbs.
Here in the shadows, we reminisce,
And create new tales—what a bliss!

Notes on the Fridge

A note from Mom, a grocery list,
But Dad's doodles just can't be missed.
He draws a duck in a silly hat,
Next to a shopping cart with a sprawl like that!

Sticky notes of things to do,
But little sis just added "floo"
With stars and hearts, a funny plight,
Making chores sound like sheer delight!

"Dinner at six," then "Oops, just kidding!"
The fridge becomes our place for bidding.
We wager laughs with every bite,
Who knew home could taste so bright?

In this patchwork of family lore,
Our fridge is where we truly score.
With jumbled chaos, love does blend,
In notes and quirks, we find the trend!

Patterns of Our Lives

Stains on the carpet, a vivid view,
Chocolate fingers, a sticky crew.
The cat hides from the chaos, oh my,
As we trip over toys, we laugh till we cry.

Matching pajamas, that's a joke,
Parents sport patterns, like a cloak.
We claim it's style, a family thing,
But really it's just a fun little fling.

Routines get funny when mishaps ensue,
Mixing up lunch, sardines for stew!
We learn to laugh, share a grace,
Finding joy in every little space.

Life makes us twist, bend, and fold,
In these patterns, stories unfold.
With laughter guiding, we always strive,
In the quilt of our lives, love's alive!

The Fortress of Us

In the living room we gather,
With snacks that make us laugh,
Dad's jokes make the meter soar,
While Mom serves us all by half.

The dog steals a shoe or two,
We chase him round the floor,
He's king of this crazy crew,
We can't help but adore.

The fortress built with pillows high,
Cushions piled up like clouds,
We'll trap the giggles right inside,
While dodging silly crowds.

Dinner's served with a funny twist,
The pasta looks like art,
Together in this blissful mess,
In laughter, we're set apart.

A Homecoming Poem.

Knock, knock, who's at the door?
Oh wait, it's just my cat,
She greets me like I'm a star,
With a meow and a pat.

Mom hands me a plate so wide,
Filled with cookies and cheer,
"Who needs dinner? Have a bite!"
I'll start my diet next year.

Dad greets me with his old joke,
"Did you bring your suitcase?"
I roll my eyes but can't help laugh,
At his smiling, goofy face.

The warmth of home is bright and bold,
With chaos all around,
Yet in this funny, warm embrace,
True happiness is found.

Whispers in the Attic

The attic holds our dusty dreams,
With treasures piled so high,
A ghost who wears my mom's old coat,
And sighs out loud, "Oh My!"

We stumble on the squeaky stairs,
Like ninjas on a quest,
Uncovering the strangest things,
A ticklish poltergeist dressed best.

A box of photos tells the tale,
Of wacky, wild times gone by,
We laugh, we point, we reminisce,
As the years continue to fly.

In the attic, we become kids,
With stories spun in glee,
Our whispers echo through the beams,
Creating our own history.

Heartbeats in the Hallway

In the hallway, footfalls dance,
A parade of silly sights,
Mom with her slippers, Dad with socks,
Like clowns in kitchen lights.

Siblings dash with laughter loud,
Like tornadoes in the fridge,
"Who took my last snack?" we shout,
While dodging kitchen midge.

The echo of a playful race,
Makes the heart feel light,
As we skirt around the corners,
In our home, pure delight.

With every heartbeat, joy unfolds,
In every nook and cranny,
Together, we gather the laughter,
In this home, we are all zany.

The Umbrella that Keeps Us Dry

When raindrops dance like tiny mice,
   We grab our brolly; what a price!
   It flips and flops, a wonky ride,
   But together we laugh and glide.

The dog barks loud, he's soaked and bold,
   He thinks he's fierce, or so we're told.
   In puddles, splashes, chuckles bloom,
   As we all dash, hoping for room.

A storm can't dampen our inside glee,
   For games of tag are wild and free.
Our rooftop shields from nature's show,
While jokes fly high, as raindrops flow.

So here we stand, a circus band,
   With squirrels waltzing, making plans.
Laughter rises like a good pie's crust,
   Together we shine, in fun we trust.

A Mosaic of Memories

Each captured smile, a quirky frame,
From family gatherings to puppy games.
Spilled drinks, and laughter, and burnt pie trust,
A gallery of chaos that's truly a must.

Old socks as puppets, our silly art,
A mural of madness that warms the heart.
With mismatched chairs, a wobbly scene,
Our home's a place where it's safe to dream.

The fridge is a canvas, with notes galore,
"Don't eat the leftovers," then noms floor to floor!
Each crayon doodle tells tales of cheer,
In this madcap home, there's nothing to fear.

So here we reside with giggles in store,
Creating a tapestry, forever more.
Every quirk and blunder finds love in our nest,
A colorful patchwork where all feel blessed.

The Flicker of Home

A toaster's pop is a morning cheer,
It sings to us, 'Hey, breakfast is here!'
That lamp's loose bulb? A disco ball,
We groove through the spaces, hear laughter call.

The cat on the counter, an acrobat pro,
Dishing out chaos with just one toe.
His nap's interrupted, the dishes alike,
Beneath the chaos, there's love we strike.

Flickering shadows chase up the wall,
While second-hand treasures, they answer the call.
Each little echo, each quirky creak,
Makes our home warm, a cozy mystique.

As evening sets in, we gather, we jest,
Our hearts are twinkling, truly blessed.
In every situation, the humor gets sown,
In the flickers and giggles, we find our own.

Beneath the Surface of Familiarity

Underneath the calm, the stir begins,
A dance of antics where fun never thins.
The carpet cushions all upturned shoes,
In this wild realm, we'll never lose!

The walls have ears that secretly grin,
As tales of mishaps and joy spin.
The couch has seen our bickering wars,
Yet holds us close, through laughter's roars.

Sticky notes litter the fridge with flair,
"Don't forget the cake!" and "Who took my hair?"
Each note a reminder of quirks we share,
In this bonkers bubble, love fills the air.

So here we thrive, amidst the fray,
As we tumble and stumble through this play.
In the layers of laughter, our bond we'll weave,
A tapestry of silly, in which we believe.

As the Night Falls

As the sun dips low and the shadows play,
The cat takes the couch, the dog steals the sway.
Grandma's snoring echoes, a deep rumbling sound,
While socks and odd toys are scattered around.

The fridge hums a tune, our late-night delight,
Leftovers calling, as we sneak through the night.
Cereals and cookies, we gather in glee,
The kitchen's a party—just you, cat, and me.

Late-night laughter floats through the hall,
As we tell crazy tales, one after the fall.
The clock strikes twelve, that's our cue to stop,
But we burst into giggles, we just can't drop.

Pajamas askew, we head off to bed,
With whispers of mischief dancing in our head.
Tomorrow will bring more antics anew,
As we craft our adventures, just me and you.

The Folded Laundry of Love

In the corner piled high, the laundry does grow,
A mountain of socks, and who knows what's below?
Each shirt tells a story, each wrinkle a laugh,
Like grandpa's old jokes, each hem a new gaffe.

The kids play dress-up in clothes fresh from the wash,
A cape made of towels, they dash and they posh.
With mismatched socks, they claim it's a trend,
While I quietly wonder if this will all end.

Static cling dances, a clingy affair,
As I wish for machines to take up the wear.
But love's in the fluff, and joy's in the fold,
Each piece an adventure, a memory told.

So we laugh as we sort through the vibrant array,
With "who wore this last?" being asked in the fray.
Our home, it's a circus, with clothes flying high,
The folded laundry of love, like a cloud in the sky.

Voices at the Dinner Table

Gathered around, the table is set,
With platters of food, and some friends we forget.
Mom tells a tale of the time we got lost,
While dad tries to prove that his dishes are tossed.

Siblings start bickering over who took the bread,
While grandma just chuckles, her face lightly red.
"Pass the potatoes!" "You've had them before!"
Oh, the tales and the laughter, who could want more?

The dog sits below, with his eyes sweetly gleamed,
Plotting his scoop of a morsel, it seemed.
"Just one little bite!" calls our little one's plea,
While dad rolls his eyes with a sight full of glee.

We toast with our cups filled with stories and cheer,
As the clock slows down, we all stay near.
Each voice in the mix, a chorus so bright,
Our dinner table dancing into the night.

A Lullaby of Memories

Under the blankets, a chorus of snores,
As I weave through the memories, like old wooden floors.

The giggles at dusk, the mischief of noon,
The dance-offs in PJs, our own little tune.

Mom's spicy stew and dad's grilling flair,
Each flavor a story, a reminder laid bare.
A lullaby tugs gently at heartstrings aglow,
Whispers of laughter in the soft afterglow.

Caught between dreams, like fireflies in flight,
The glow of their laughter keeps shadows from night.
The tales once told weave through twilight so sweet,
Cradled in joy, it's our world, our retreat.

So here's to the moments, the mishaps, the charms,
The warmth of our home as it opens its arms.
When night falls in hush and the day's fits and starts,
I'll hum this sweet lullaby, the song of our hearts.

Family Portraits Framed in Time

In a frame, we all stand still,
Mom's hairdo, a towering hill.
Dad with snacks, in hand a treat,
Sister's smile, a crooked feat.

Uncle Joe, with pants too tight,
A captured moment, quite a sight.
Grandma's cat, the guest of fame,
Whiskers twitch when they hear her name.

A family tree, we love to climb,
Branches bending, oh, the crime.
A vibrant laugh, a silly pose,
Captured hearts, with all our woes.

Through each portrait, laughter flows,
In every glance, silly knows.
A legacy of joy we keep,
In memories, we laugh and leap.

Whispered Hopes and Fears

In the kitchen, secrets brew,
Whispered hopes on fancy stew.
Burning toast, a smoky fright,
Dad just laughs, "It's gourmet night!"

With every wink, a tale unfolds,
Of dreams and plans, and daring bolds.
Fears of spiders, mice that squeak,
Mom shouts, "No one's here but a leak!"

With tension high, our giggles soar,
A comedy show behind closed door.
"Who forgot to take the trash?"
"Oh, that's right, it was a splash!"

In whispered laughs, we find our way,
Through kitchen chaos, come what may.
Hopes knitted tight, like Grandma's yarn,
We stitch our lives with silly charm.

The Magic of Ordinary Days

In the mundane, magic hides,
Spinning stories, like roller slides.
A spilled drink, a twirl and swish,
Grumpy cat, he made a wish.

Socks mismatched, it's our new style,
Mom's grumpy face, but then a smile.
Chasing bubbles, floating high,
Dad's dad jokes make the doves cry!

Laundry mountains, peaks of chaos,
Folding skills, we'll never gloss.
"Who's wearing these?" we laugh and tease,
A family puzzle, if you please!

In each ordinary little thing,
We find the joy that laughter brings.
Every day a dance, a song,
In our hearts is where we belong.

Light Through the Kitchen Window

Sunlight spills on the floor,
Dust bunnies dance, wanting more.
The cat leaps up, a leap of faith,
Chasing shadows, it's her wraith!

Mom's baking bread, the smell so sweet,
Dad sneaks crumbs, a little treat.
Kids play hide and seek in beams,
Muffled giggles, bursting seams.

Through the glass, the world's aglow,
Each golden ray brings a show.
Breakfast chaos, we all convene,
With sticky fingers, we make a scene.

A dance in light, a joyful mess,
In every corner, love's excess.
Through that window, we wave and grin,
This is where our tales begin.

Hidden Corners and Secret Spaces

In the attic, dust bunnies play,
Chasing each other through hidden hay.
Forgotten toys in darkened spots,
A war of action figures and cats.

Mom's old shoes with holes galore,
Pretend they're portals to lands we adore.
Under the couch, a sock brigade,
Plotting their escape, a grand charade!

A hidden fort made of blanket swirls,
Where pirates and princesses trade their pearls.
Mismatched cushions form lumpy thrones,
With brave adventures and playful groans.

Lurking in drawers with papers piled,
Crayons and glitter from when we were wild.
These secret spaces sing sweet rhymes,
Crafting memories across the times.

Flickering Candlelight

A candle winks at the midnight hour,
Casting shadows that bravely tower.
The cat's silhouette, a stealthy ghost,
Prowls through the dark, playing host to toast.

Mom's frying pan sings a sizzling tune,
As kids sneak snacks beneath the moon.
The scent of popcorn fills the air,
While laughter crackles, oh what a flair!

Jars of jellybeans in vibrant hues,
Make bedtime battles of the sugar blues.
A late-night heist, stealthy and bright,
Sneaking past parents in candlelight.

With giggles and whispers, the night will flee,
Every flicker holds a story, you see.
In the glow, mischief dances slight,
Creating legends of glorious fright!

Stories Woven in Silence

In the quiet, whispers float and twirl,
Secrets dance like leaves in a whirl.
A grumpy chair that creaks with glee,
Telling tales of tea stains and jubilee.

The clock ticks loud, but time stands still,
While shadows gather on window sill.
Uncle Joe spills stories, half-truths that jest,
Of adventures in socks that never rest!

Footsteps echo in the hallway shy,
While ghostly giggles drift on by.
The puppy's snores, a symphony sweet,
Compose the sound of homecoming feats.

Beneath the stares of portraits hung,
The stories cling like songs unsung.
In silent corners, the laughter grows,
As the moon peeks in, and the tension slows.

Nooks of Nostalgia

In a nook where the sunlight pours,
Dust motes dance like fairy wars.
An old rocking chair whispers and rocks,
Recalling the tales of time-worn clocks.

Crayons scattered like rainbows spilled,
Artistic creations that laughter thrilled.
Paintings of stick figures and wild trees,
Evoke chuckles with a gentle breeze.

Granddad's old hat, with feathers and flair,
Sits in a corner, with stories to share.
Dressed like a pirate or a dapper gent,
In fond recollection, our time is spent.

The smell of cookies with laughter baked,
Echoes of recipes that memories make.
In these nooks, the heart finds peace,
As moments freeze, and worries cease.

The Shelter of Memories

In the attic, boxes lay,
Filled with toys from yesterday.
A dusty bear with missing eye,
Winks at me from way up high.

Grandpa's hats all stacked in rows,
One's too small—it's on my toes.
The memories dance, swirl, and spin,
As I ponder where to begin.

Mom's bright laugh, the burnt-up cake,
The wild cat, a tiny quake.
Home's a circus, quite the show,
With every secret we both know.

Old shoes stored with dusty pride,
The garden gnome who likes to hide.
Through time's lens, we poke and prod,
Finding joy in the great facade.

Beyond the Front Door

When guests arrive, the doors swing wide,
In they come, with gifts inside.
A rubber chicken, what a sight,
Causes laughter, pure delight.

The rug's a trap for clumsy feet,
Each entrance makes for quite a feat.
"Watch your step!" I always cry,
But that's the fun, we all comply.

Beneath the porch, raccoons await,
Plotting mischief, isn't it great?
They steal my lunch as I abscond,
But "No worries!"—we always respond.

Wacky hats adorn the walls,
As clingy friends make silly calls.
With each embrace, we seem to thrive,
Outside adventures keep us alive.

A Tapestry of Comfort

The couch is soft, but it won't hold,
My cat, she thinks she's very bold.
She claims a spot right on my lap,
While I just sit, a cozy trap.

The blankets pile like clouds of fun,
In every color, all come undone.
They wrap around like a warm hug,
Each corner's a little snug bug.

The kitchen smells of burnt toast fate,
With garlic bread on the dinner plate.
I try to whisk, but eggs do fly,
Who knew they'd land on the dog nearby?

Together we dine on half-cooked stew,
With winking faces, who knew it's true?
A mess can feel like pure delight,
In this goofy, love-filled night.

Where the Heart Finds Rest

A creaky bed, it knows too well,
Of whispered dreams and tales to tell.
It grumbles loud when I sit down,
But soothes me too, in each soft frown.

The mirror reflects my sleepy face,
With toothpaste splatters, a funny trace.
Fuzzy slippers, mismatched on toes,
Bring giggles each morning as the sun glows.

The pets all snore, a chorus grand,
With one eye open, they try to stand.
A pillow fort is my retreat,
Where bedtime stories can't be beat.

So in this place, we laugh and rest,
With funny quirks that are the best.
Home's a puzzle, a joyous mess,
Where love grows strong, I must confess.

A Gathering of Hearts

In the kitchen, the laughter spills,
A dance of spoons and joyful thrills.
Mom sings loud, and Dad can't keep time,
As the dog suddenly joins in the rhyme.

Uncle Joe tells tales that are slightly off,
A ghost in a cupboard that makes us scoff.
A tickle war starts with a cheeky grin,
And Grandpa's lost his glasses again.

Cousins collide in a roguish chase,
Not just for snacks, but also for space.
Who hid the cookies? Don't point at me!
It's chaos, but oh, what fun to be free.

As the sun sets, stories take flight,
From the living room echo, laughter so bright.
Our hearts bound tight like a funny old tune,
In this circus of love, we'll gather again soon.

Garden of Childhood

In the backyard, where wildflowers grow,
We crafted castles with mud, you know.
A slide made of cardboard, our secret base,
A kingdom of giggles in every place.

The swing set swayed like a pirate's ship,
With daring leaps and no fear of a trip.
We played hide-and-seek with the sun as our guide,
In our garden of dreams, where joy would abide.

A catnip jungle, big trees to climb,
With bees buzzing tales that dance in rhyme.
Crouched in the bushes, alive with our schemes,
We were kings and queens in our wildest dreams.

But time is a thief, it shuffles away,
Yet in every flower, a memory will stay.
In this garden where laughter has sown,
We still bloom brightly, never alone.

Rooms Filled with Unseen Histories

In the attic, where shadows do play,
Old boxes hold secrets from yesterday.
A teddy bear, worn but still bright,
Whispers stories under starry night.

The creaky floorboards, they groan with glee,
As stories of triumph dance silently.
Grandma's old dresses, a dainty parade,
Each crinkle a tale, perfectly laid.

The hallway echoes with footsteps of yore,
As whispers of laughter slip through the door.
Family portraits in frames of old wood,
Smile down at us, in siblinghood good.

But there's that one sock—where could it roam?
It must have a life far away from home.
In these rooms, both silly and wise,
Stories live on, and we are the prize.

The Weight of a Family Shoe

In the hallway, two shoes sit side by side,
One's big as a boat, the other, a guide.
They've marched through laughter and blunders galore,
Filling this house with tales to explore.

A toddler's step, wobbly and sweet,
Then off to the living room's playtime retreat.
But find that lost shoe under the bed?
It's found its way home, by mischief led!

Dad's shoes have a story, the squeak and the scuff,
They've walked through the mud, and they think they're tough.
Yet here they just cradle some old, dusty fun,
While Mom's tiny heels tap in the run.

So we giggle and muck about, trip and swoon,
In a world of shoes, we'll waltz to the moon.
With every misplaced shoe, a story does sprout,
What fun it is just to laugh and hang out!

Moments in a Sunbeam

A cat sprawls wide, claiming my chair,
Sunbeams dance with a playful flare.
I trip on socks, my dog gives a grin,
Life's little mishaps, where joy begins.

Coffee spills on the floor with a splash,
My toddler giggles, making a dash.
With each little laugh, the chaos flows,
In silly moments, the happiness grows.

Off-key singing in the shower flows,
The curtain's my stage as the melody grows.
The shampoo bottle cheers, bubbles collide,
In this joyful mess, we full-heartedly abide.

Chasing the dust bunnies, we compete,
My pet stands ready, a speedy feat.
With laughter echoing through every room,
In golden light, there's always room for bloom.

Reflections in an Old Mirror

Staring back is a face of surprises,
Old mirror gleams with a hundred disguises.
A hairdo resembling a bird's nest show,
Like a comedy act, it steals the show.

A wrinkle appears, a giggle ensues,
Could it be age, or just bad news?
I poke at my cheek, make a silly face,
In the mirror's reflection, I find my place.

Each night brings new tales etched in glass,
With every chortle, I let moments pass.
I strike a pose, the mirror just shakes,
With laughter echoing, the canvas it makes.

The mirror knows secrets, both funny and bold,
Of socks on my hands and pajamas of gold.
Together we chuckle, in this old nook,
Here lies my story, just take a look.

Dreams Locked in a Drawer

In a drawer lies a treasure untold,
Old toys and scribbles, a memory unfold.
Each crayon drawing, a time capsule waits,
Recalling wild dreams that crayon creates.

The mismatched socks dance a silly jig,
A stuffed bear whispers, 'You're still a kid.'
Nostalgic giggles echo from deep,
Unlocking a past where joy falls asleep.

Forgotten wishes tucked well out of sight,
A spaceship made from a cardboard knight.
With each little find, the fun reappears,
In the drawer's embrace, laughter steers.

So we rummage through dreams, like a treasure hunt,
Every little giggle is a joyous stunt.
With each piece unearthed, the spirit does soar,
In this whimsy world, we're forever four.

Rainsong on the Roof

Pitter-patter sings on the shingles above,
A symphony played by the skies we love.
The cat jumps high with a startled meow,
As puddles perform their own curtain bow.

In rubber boots, we splash without care,
Dance like nobody's watching, everywhere.
Raindrops burst with a giggle divine,
Each drop a note, like a whimsical line.

Doorframes become stages for mischief and flair,
With waterlogged shoes, our artistic affair.
Raincoats twirl under gray, clouded skies,
In this soaking canvas, our joy never dies.

So let the rain pour, we'll dance with the flow,
In soggy delight, our happiness grows.
Rainsong above, we hum along too,
In this splashy ballad, the world feels brand new.

Cracks in the Old Floor

There's a crack in the floor, I trip over it now,
The cat rolls its eyes, like it's seen this somehow.
I jump and I stumble, arms flailing in air,
While the dog just sits back, grinning without care.

Grandpa tells stories of days gone so grand,
When folks would just dance in this old, creaky land.
But I think all the cracks are just portals to fun,
Inviting mishaps that cannot be outdone.

I swear that the floor has a mind of its own,
It hides all my slippers, like it's a prank zone.
Each time I step lightly, I hear creaks and groans,
Like an old man is snoring in a room full of bones.

Yet laughter erupts when I fall with a thud,
These cracks bring us joy, like old jokes turned to blood.
A dance down the hall, a humorous plight,
In this crooked old house, every moment feels right.

The Heart's Safe Haven

The fridge hums a tune that I know by heart,
It's the anthem of snacks, and I'm ready to start.
With pizza and leftovers, a feast just for me,
I pull open the door, it's a sight to see!

Mom hides in the pantry, counting her treats,
With a sly grin, she's hoarding sweets.
But the cookies are friendly; they whisper and call,
Join us for munching! Who cares if you fall?

The couch is a fortress, all cushions and fluff,
A landscape of comfort, it's totally tough.
With remote control battles, we're kings of the night,
And victory dances, when we finally fight!

Here laughter echoes, and the moments are grand,
Even spilt drinks are met with a hand.
Family and fun in this haven we've made,
It's the heart of our home, where joy won't fade!

Timeless Treasures

In the attic, I found my old stuffed-up bear,
With a button for an eye and a patch of his hair.
He's ready for stories and tea party games,
Dust bunnies join in, as he calls out their names.

There's a box full of hats, each sillier than last,
With feathers and sparkles, they burst out so fast!
We play make-believe, a royal parade,
Where fashion is reckless, yet joyfully made.

A mix of old socks and some marbles with zest,
Are the treasures of childhood, a funny old fest.
We build up a castle, with pillows as walls,
And launch a brave knight, from soft, bouncy halls!

Laughter collides with nostalgia so bright,
As we reenact tales till we run out of light.
These treasures remind us of moments so fine,
In the attic of laughter, where hearts intertwine.

Soundtrack of Everyday Living

The toaster pops up, it sings a loud tune,
While the dog howls along, a quirky raccoon.
The kettle whistles, like a bird in the skies,
As I shuffle and dance, what a morning surprise!

Napkins crinkle like a band in their prime,
While I juggle the plates, it's all about time.
Spoons hit the pot with a clink and a bang,
As my dance turns to chaos, the laughter just sang.

Oh, the fridge plays a melody of veggies and jams,
Each item a note in our family programs.
The clock ticks away, somehow beating along,
To the rhythm of life, we all sing the song.

In this symphony sweet, each moment we share,
Is a laughter-filled chorus, in the cool evening air.
Our home is a concert, no need for a stage,
Just a sprinkle of fun, on the bright daily page.

Stories Within the Walls

In corners where dust bunnies might play,
Whispering secrets of yesterday.
Socks with holes on the laundry doom,
Argue loudly in the living room.

The cat thinks he rules with a whimsical grace,
While pillows form fortresses, a soft, cozy space.
The fridge hums gently, a buddy for snacks,
While the vacuum's a monster that silently attacks.

Every family photo tells a weird tale,
Of Uncle Bob's dance with a giant snail.
The dog's goofy grin and his clumsy prance,
Set the scene for a mishap of every failed dance.

Through laughter and chaos, we build a nest,
In the chaos of warmth, we find our best.
The walls might be quiet, but oh what they know,
Each nook holds a giggle, a high-flying show.

Emotions in the Eaves

The attic's a wild place for dreams to soar,
Where elves consider how to fix the floor.
Dust motes are fairies on a glittering spree,
While mice play chess with grand strategy.

Old shoes and hats, stories untold,
Of someone's childhood that never grows old.
Nostalgia creeps in like a ticklish breeze,
Making us chuckle, then laugh 'til we wheeze.

The eaves are alive with buzz and with joy,
To hear the old tales, oh what a ploy!
Each creak and each groan has a story to share,
Of a vanished sock or a family scare.

While mom's calling down, 'Get your shoes off the chair!'

We're staging a heist without any care.
Each moment of mayhem, a cherished refrain,
In our little kingdom, where laughter's the gain.

A Quilt of Togetherness

Under this quilt stitched with giggles and glee,
Lies a treasure of stories, like honey from bees.
Each patch a reminder of laughter and fun,
Of pillow fights won and of race to the sun.

Grandma's old slippers are flung near the fire,
As she shares wild tales that never tire.
The popcorn bowl dances, it jumps and it spills,
While we argue who's turning the next set of thrills.

Cousin Larry's snoring could rival a train,
But we stifle our laughs, a collective refrain.
With every small poke, a ripple of cheer,
A saga of silliness we'll hold dear.

As shadows grow long and the giggles subside,
We settle in close, with no thoughts to hide.
In this cozy patchwork, our hearts intertwine,
A tapestry stitched by love, oh how divine!

Hearthstone Reverie

By the hearth, we gather, with marshmallows in hand,
Imagining adventures across distant lands.
A game of charades with the dog as the star,
He barks loudly—'I'm an eagle from afar.'

The fireplace crackles with stories untold,
Of the golden days when we were all bold.
Silly tales of giants who stole dad's last fries,
And of the mysterious sock thief in disguise.

Mom's making hot cocoa, a frothy delight,
As we compete on who can stay up all night.
A contest of giggles, a battle of cheer,
Where who keeps it together is way more sincere.

When bedtime arrives, oh the groans that arise,
With secret conspiracies and twinkling eyes.
The hearthstone's our stage for a delightful show,
As we drift off to dreamland, where funny tales flow.

www.ingramcontent.com/pod-product-compliance
Lightning Source LLC
Chambersburg PA
CBHW051731290426
43661CB00122B/222